Boise State College Western Writers Series   Number 7

Owen Wister

By Richard W. Etulain

Idaho State University

Editors: Wayne Chatterton
James H. Maguire

Business Manager:
James Hadden

Cover Design and Illustration
by Arny Skov, Copyright 1973

Boise State College, Boise, Idaho

Printed in the United States of America by
The Caxton Printers, Ltd.
Caldwell, Idaho

Owen Wister

Owen Wister

The summer of 1885 was a turning point in the life of Owen Wister. Approaching age twenty-five, Wister was a frustrated young man. He could not settle down, he was undecided on a career, and he suffered from extreme nervous tension. Wister went to the West to elude his difficulties. The summer in Wyoming was just what the doctor ordered. Wister's nervous problems disappeared, and he entered Harvard Law School in the fall. More important, the West caught Wister's attention; it provided several summers of vacation and eventually supplied material for his most significant writing. From his contact with the American West, Owen Wister produced numerous short stories and two novels, one of which—*The Virginian*—proved to be a model for much fiction written about the West.

Wister was born July 14, 1860, in Germantown, a suburb of Philadelphia. He was the only child of Owen Jones and Sarah (Butler) Wister. His mother was the daughter of Fanny Kemble, the noted actress, and Pierce Butler, grandson of the Pierce Butler who served in the Constitutional Convention. Their daughter, Sarah, inherited her parents' aristocratic bearing and independence of mind, and in particular her mother's devotion to the arts. Throughout her life, Sarah Butler Wister enjoyed being a woman among women; she spoke French and Italian fluently, played the piano, and wrote articles for leading magazines. She enjoyed social gatherings and counted among her close friends such men as the novelist Henry James. Mrs. Wister indulged her interest in the arts and passed on that interest to her son. They began corresponding before he was ten, and they continued this weekly correspondence until her death in 1908. The letters are full of advice—what plays to see, what books to read, and what to think about what he saw and read. Wister leaned heavily on his mother's advice (though he argued with her opinions frequently). She was clearly *the* intellectual influence on his formative years.

Wister never spoke much about his father. Owen Jones Wister was a prominent physician whose ancestors settled in Pennsylvania. Though much less interested in social gatherings than was his wife, Wister's father was known for his wit and love of humor. His early correspondence with Wister indicates a father willing to provide a fine education for his son but also a man who wanted his offspring to find an honest and financially-rewarding occupation. He was dissatisfied with Wister's early choice of music as a career and encouraged him toward banking or law. Less indulgent than Wister's mother, he wanted his only son to select a career that would neither embarrass the family nor fail to support him.

During his early years, Wister traveled a great deal. He attended a boarding school in Switzerland for three months; he spent a year at a school in Hofwyl, Switzerland, while his parents traveled and visited with Fanny Kemble in Europe; and he lived in Hereford, England, for a year with his maternal aunt and her husband. After returning home from Europe in 1873, the Wisters sent Owen to St. Paul's School in Concord, New Hampshire.

Wister was a student at St. Paul's for five years. This prestigious New Hampshire institution, modeled after English prep schools, was headed by an Episcopalian clergyman and emphasized a strictly controlled curriculum based on the classics. Wister was a good student, besides being active in several organizations. He played a prominent role in the school's library association, joined the choir, found time to compose a few tunes, and even thought of writing an opera. His first published story, "Down in a Diving Bell," appeared in the school magazine in 1873, and later he became editor of the magazine, to which he also contributed essays and poems.

In the fall of 1878 Wister enrolled at Harvard. As George Watkins has pointed out, three facets of Wister's life at Harvard stand out: his "circle of friends . . . , his literary activities, and his musical studies" ("Owen Wister and the American West," p. 31). While at Harvard, Wister met, among others, William Dean Howells, Oliver Wendell Holmes, Jr., Henry Cabot Lodge, and Theodore Roosevelt. He belonged to honored organizations like the Porcelian Club and the Hasty Pudding Club, and he continued his literary interests by writing for school magazines. His "The New Swiss Family Robinson" ran for seven issues of the *Lampoon* during late 1882 and appeared later that year as his first book. But his major was music (he had already decided to become a composer), and it was to this interest that he devoted most of his energy. He wrote the lyrics for several musical performances, and during his senior year he wrote the words and music and performed in a Hasty Pudding production of *Dido and Aeneas*. He was elected to Phi Beta Kappa and was graduated *summa cum laude* in the spring of 1882.

Still convinced that he ought to be a composer, Wister departed for Europe the following summer. In August, armed with one of many letters of recommendation that always opened doors for Wister, he visited Franz Liszt in Beyreuth. The aging pianist responded enthusiastically to one of Wister's compositions. At the end of the year in Paris, Wister wished to stay on, but his father requested that he return home to take a position with Major Henry Lee Higginson. He returned, but because there was no opening at Lee, Higginson, and Company, he was forced to take a position computing interest at Union Safe Deposit Vaults in Boston.

Wister soon tired of his job. Only his association with Howells and other acquaintances in the newly-founded Tavern Club seemed to revive his spirits. Wister's frustrations grew, his health worsened, and he quit his job. Meanwhile, he was trying his hand at writing. With his cousin Langdon Mitchell, Wister produced a long novel titled *A Wise Man's Son*. Then the manuscript was shipped off to Howells, who advised that it not be submitted to a publisher. Howells thought the novel too realistic, too shocking for the American public. As he put it, "a whole fig tree couldn't cover one of the woman characters" (*Owen Wister Out West*, p. 11). So in the spring of 1885 Wister's life seemed a series of frustrations. He had not found an occupation, in spite of paternal pressures, and his musical and literary endeavors had not come to fruition. So Wister went to the West at the advice of his relative, Dr. S. Weir Mitchell.

The reactions that Wister recorded in his first Western journals were like those of a convict seeing the outside world for the first time in many years. Wister was enthusiastic—he was ecstatic:

> One must come to the West to realize what one may have most probably believed all one's life long—that it is a very much bigger place than the East, and the future America is just bubbling and seething in bare legs and pinafores here. I don't wonder a man never comes back [East] after he has once been here for a few years. (*Owen Wister Out West*, pp. 29-30)

His first Western experiences in Wyoming worked the changes Wister needed: "This existence," he wrote, "is heavenly in its monotony and sweetness. Wish I were going to do it every summer. I'm beginning to be able to feel I'm something of an animal and not a stinking brain alone" (*Owen Wister Out West*, p. 32).

And he did return nearly every summer. After the first trek

westward in 1885 he made fourteen others before 1900. These trips promised a respite from the complexities that seemed to close in on him. So the excursions westward were more than sight-seeing tours; they were antidotes for the perplexities that were eating at his psyche.

Returning home in 1885 after his first trip into the West, Wister enrolled in Harvard Law School in the fall. He was graduated in 1888, and a year later he moved into the Philadelphia offices of Frances Rawle to practice law. Admitted to the bar in 1890, he meanwhile continued his other interests. He tried to write operas, and he continued to travel into the West. Even as he prepared for law he thought seriously about becoming a writer. As early as 1889 he began taking copious notes about his Western experiences. By the summer of 1891 he went to Wyoming to gather regional materials for "a great fat book about the whole thing [the West]." Gradually Wister was moving in the direction of becoming an author—and the West offered the most interesting materials for his writing. Though he had written about music and had turned out several poems and other fiction, he was now on the verge of becoming a *Western* writer.

In his biography of Roosevelt, Wister explains the often-cited origins of his first Western tale. One evening in the early fall of 1891 he was dining with his friend Walter Furness. As Wister bewailed the fact that no one was "saving the sagebrush for American literature" before it went the way of the forty-niner, the Mississippi steamboat, and other Western experiences, he decided that he would have to do the job. He told Furness: "Walter, I'm going to try it myself! . . . I'm going to start this minute." That evening he retreated upstairs at the Philadelphia Club and began "Hank's Woman." By January of 1892 he had completed this tale and a second one titled "How Lin McLean Went East." Harper's bought both stories. Wister was on the trail headed upward.

Now the Western trips had a different purpose. Now he

traveled as a writer looking for material. He sent for books about Western speech and customs, he badgered his friends to share their Western experiences, and he took copious notes— all for the purpose of working these raw materials into his tales. In 1894, Harper's gave added assurance to his decision to become a Western writer when the firm sent him into the West to write a series of "short stories of Western Adventure. Each must be a thrilling story, having its ground in a real incident, though you are left free scope for imaginative treatment. . . . We wish in this series to portray certain features of Western life which are now rapidly disappearing with the progress of civilization" (Owen Wister Papers, Library of Congress, Henry Alden to Wister, July 14, 1893).

Wister's Western writings began to appear more regularly. In 1894, *Harper's* published eight pieces, then five the next year. By late 1895 his first collection of Western tales—*Red Men and White*—was ready for publication. Though Wyoming was still his favorite Western retreat, he traveled into Texas, into other parts of the Southwest, into the Northwest, and down the Pacific Coast. Most often his tales appeared in *Harper's* before they were put together in book form. Published in 1897, *Lin McLean* was advertised as a novel, but was actually a series of short episodes strung together in book form. A second collection of stories—*The Jimmyjohn Boss and Other Stories*—was published in 1900.

If Wister's trips helped to solve his personal problems, and to provide him with an occupation, the other event that gave his life certainty was his marriage in 1898 to Mary Channing Wister. A distant cousin, she too had been born and reared in Philadelphia, and Wister had known her for several years. Ten years younger than Wister, and a descendant of William Ellery Channing, Mary was a talented musician and a woman of good health and steady nerves. It was an excellent match, for their temperaments and interests were complementary. Purchasing a home in Philadelphia, the Wisters settled down to a tranquil life. Their family grew to six children—three boys and three girls—before Mrs. Wister died in childbirth in 1913.

The tranquility and satisfaction that arose out of his happy marriage and the added responsibilities of a growing family urged Wister back to his writing desk. He completed a biography of Ulysses S. Grant in 1900, and then in 1901 he began serious work on the novel about the Virginian. In January of 1902 the Wisters moved to Charleston, South Carolina (the site of their happy honeymoon in 1898), and Wister worked long hours juxtaposing earlier stories about the Virginian and new sections that he was writing. Wister knew he had written a good book, but he was not prepared for what happened.

The Virginian galloped to the top of the best seller list and remained there for several months. The novel was reprinted fifteen times within the first eight months and sold more than any other book during 1902-03. More pleasing to Wister was the unanimous praise of his friends, reviewers, and critics. Even President Roosevelt, to whom the book was dedicated, wrote an enthusiastic letter of congratulations. At forty-two Wister was a famous man. He was besieged by fan letters, autograph hunters, and requests to undertake all sorts of writing projects. *The Virginian* had captured the attention of many Americans who hungered and thirsted after a frontier that would continue and would not be engulfed by the tidal wave of urbanism and industrialism that seemed to threaten the nation at the turn of the century. Wister shared these misgivings, and his novel reflected predominant feelings of the Progressive Era. His cowboy hero, something of a combination of Theodore Roosevelt and Andrew Jackson, became a symbol for his age. Wister never again came as close to mirroring contemporary American feelings as he did in 1902.

The financial success of *The Virginian* and the tranquility of his successful marriage seemed to lull Wister into inactivity.

Although he published a superficial yarn of Harvard undergraduates (*Philosophy 4*) in 1903 and a full-length novel (*Lady Baltimore*) in 1906, he seemed uninterested in trying to assault again the Parnassus of Western literature. Increasingly his interests turned inward (to his family and to American politics) and eastward to Europe. Soon after the outbreak of the First World War, he wrote several pamphlets and books supporting the allied cause. Among these were *The Pentecost of Calamity* (1915), *A Straight Deal, or the Ancient Grudge* (1920), and *Neighbors Henceforth* (1922).

For Wister his later years were ones of relaxation and of resting on his laurels. He served on the Harvard Board of Overseers (1912-18, 1919-25), became a member of the American Academy of Arts and Letters and an honorary fellow of the Royal Society of Literature, and was given honorary degrees from several universities. The few Western pieces that he turned out in the late twenties were shot through with nostalgia, as the title of his last collection indicates—*When West Was West* (1928). The same year his collected works were published in eleven volumes. In 1930 Wister wrote his final book, *Roosevelt: The Story of a Friendship*.

Wister never remarried after the death of his wife. His life more and more centered on the activities of his children, his Philadelphia friends, and his cultural interests in the East and Europe. Yet he was open to newer trends in literature; he was, for example, one of the first men to encourage Ernest Hemingway. But his earlier years in the West were now stored away in the treasure chest of fond memories; and so when invited to go to Wyoming in the 1930's, he refused because his life there was lost in the past. The West had changed too much. Wister died on July 21, 1938, of a cerebral hemorrhage, and was buried in North Laurel Hill Cemetery in Philadelphia.

The career of Wister as a Western writer is best seen as an effort first to comprehend the West and then to capture its essence in his fiction. Even before he published his first Western stories in 1892, Wister demonstrated in his Western journals, which he kept on each Western jaunt, his desire to know the West, to understand it so well that its flavor and mores would provide brands of authenticity for his writings. But this quest is only gradually apparent.

Wister's initial reactions to the West are those one would expect from a young man penned up with effete backgrounds and stifled with numerous frustrations. His West was like that of Easterners such as Theodore Roosevelt and Frederic Remington: a place that exhibited sights and generated experiences that were in sharp contrast to Eastern genteel backgrounds. Or, to invoke another comparison, Wister's need to go West was similar to Ernest Hemingway's desire—thirty years later—to get out of Oak Park, Illinois. They both wanted to avoid restrictive elements of their environments and to prove themselves on their own. As Wister's daughter would write many years later, a trip to the West was not an unnatural undertaking. "There were a lot of expensively educated young men going West then, not seeking their fortunes or planning to settle but going for adventure. They shot elk, caught rainbow trout, and returned home" (*Owen Wister Out West*, p. xi). Wister fits this description; he came to the West as a tourist, as an onlooker, as a young man ready to embrace all he saw and to be refreshed and healed by the new sights and experiences.

The first journal entries picture a young man caught up in the scenery. Traveling through the sparsely inhabited areas of Wyoming, he enjoyed the "continual passing of green void, without any growing thing higher than a tuft of grass." Scene after scene enthralled him. "I can't possibly say how extraordinary and beautiful the valleys we've been going through are. . . . When you go for miles through the piled rocks where the fire has risen straight out of the crevices, you never see a human being—only now and then some disappearing wild animal.

It's like what scenery on the moon must be. Then suddenly you come around a turn and down into a green cut where there are horsemen and wagons and hundreds of cattle, and then it's like Genesis" (*Owen Wister Out West,* pp. 30, 31). These experiences were working the change that Wister needed. His initial reactions portray a West that is not merely a wilderness of wild animals and primitives but also a beautiful landscape and an environment that produce individualism and democracy of the sort that insured America's future.

Gradually Wister moved beyond local color description in his journals; gradually he began attempting to put together scenery and character. Step by step he commenced to show what the West did to aliens and to natives. Sometimes his responses were especially unfavorable. Western towns particularly irritated him. Whether in Wyoming, the Southwest, or the Northwest, he rarely failed to register his negative reactions to the towns he saw. Notice his description of Coulee City, Washington:

> Blowing over this waste came sudden noisome smells from the undrained filth of the town that huddled there in the midst of unlimited nothing. It is a shapeless litter of boxes, inhabited by men whose lives are an aimless drifting. . . . Coulee is too dead even for much crime. The ceaseless poker game was a cheap one, and nobody got either drunk or dangerous. People have been killed there, I believe, but not often, most likely not lately. There is but one professional woman in the whole town, and from what I heard the men say, she is a forlorn old wreck, so unsightly that even her monopoly brings no profit. In such a sordid community, this fact shows stronger than anything else how poor and torpid existence has come to be. (*Owen Wister Out West,* p. 136)

Wister knew that these surroundings were bound to shape men's characters, and he frequently wondered whether the personalities produced were not unstable ones:

> I begin to conclude from five seasons of observation that life in this negligent irresponsible wilderness tends to turn people shiftless, cruel and incompetent. I noticed in Wolcott [a Wyoming rancher with whom Wister stayed] in 1885, and I notice today, a sloth in doing anything and everything, that is born of the deceitful ease with which makeshifts answer here. (*Owen Wister Out West,* p. 112)

So here were the conflicts of Wister's West. Though the region afforded abundant opportunities for freedom, individualism, and a glimpse of primitive man in his natural surroundings, it was also a region that seemed to bring out the brutal, the vindictive, and the wanderlust in men. Much of the West, in short, might be the new Eden in which man could function as a free man, but this also meant that the slippery serpent of man's bestial nature was there too. Here, then, were raw materials for Western fiction; if a man could corral these maverick materials, and put his brand on them, he might turn out a marketable product.

Wister's first Western stories are Janus-like: they illustrate what he learned about the West since his first trip to the West in 1885, and they also introduce themes, characters, and techniques that reappear in his later writings about the West. His first two Western yarns were "Hank's Woman" and "How Lin McLean Went East." Written in the fall of 1891, they were submitted—on the advice of S. Weir Mitchell—to Henry Alden at *Harper's.* Both stories were accepted in January 1892 (Wister was paid $175.00 for the stories), and they appeared later that same year.

In "Hank's Woman" Wister utilizes the frame technique—a story within a story. "Hank's Woman" introduces a narrator and Lin McLean in the first section of the tale, and the second part is the tale of Hank and his woman that Lin shares with the first person narrator. Lin tellls of a ne'er-do-well cowpoke who suddenly marries a muscular Austrian servant girl who has been fired from her position. Most of Lin's yarn centers on Hank's ill treatment of Willomene and on her attachment to her crucifix. Tension builds, and one day Lin and his cowpoke partner return to find their camp a scene of disarray. Willomene has murdered Hank, but while dragging his body along a narrow cliff she has fallen to her death.

Wister's story is artistically weak. As George Watkins has pointed out, Wister is telling two stories: the fight between Hank and "his woman," and the frame story of Lin and the narrator. The conflict between Hank and his wife is melodramatic and contrived; it is too full of "Gothic grotesqueries." The story could have been strengthened by emphasizing the narrator's initiation into new understanding of human nature, but Wister failed to take advantage of this opportunity.

Yet the tale is not, as Watkins argues, "virtually devoid of any significant meaning" (p. 136). Throughout his career as a Western writer, Wister sought to find the meaning of the West. Frequently his search led him to compare and contrast the Western region with the East and sometimes with Europe. In "Hank's Woman" the conflict between the West and non-West is not yet very clear, but there are evidences of Wister's attempt to portray such conflicts. Lin and the narrator perceive the failures of Hank as a worthy Westerner, and they are sympathetic with Willomene's attachment to her church and to her past. The tension that could (and would) arise between the West and non-West is not well portrayed here because Wister was still uncertain what he thought about the West, how it differed from other regions, and what kind of values it might contribute to America.

In "How Lin McLean Went East" Wister seems more sure of what distinctions he wishes to make between the West and East. Lin has saved some money and decides to go East—to visit his Boston friends and family, particularly his brother Frank. Soon after he arrives, he realizes that the brother is embarrassed by Lin's ways. Lin returns to the West and tells the Bishop of Wyoming that his story is similar to that of the Biblical prodigal, except that he lacks a father. He too has squandered his funds in a far country, and now he has returned home—to the West. Wister makes clear that Lin's openness, his honesty and friendliness are Western attributes. Pitted against these positive values are Frank's pretentiousness and unfriendliness. When West and East meet in the confrontation between Lin and his brother, the West is superior. It breeds a better man, or, in the case of Lin, it pours new wine into an old wineskin.

This story is also important because it includes Wister's first extended comments about the cowboy. He is pictured as a breed apart. "He was a complete specimen of his lively and peculiar class. Cow-punchers are not a race. . . . They gallop over the face of the empty earth for a little while, and those whom rheumatism or gunpowder does not overtake, are blotted out by the course of empire, leaving no trace behind. A few wise ones return to their birthplaces, marry, and remain forever homesick for the desert sage-brush and the alkali they once cursed so heartily." Wister's picture of the cowboy is not entirely positive. As he showed earlier in his journals, the West produced noble men, but it also seemed to breed lazy, inferior men. Some of the cowboys, Wister says, "take a squaw to wife and supinely draw her rations with regularity" (p. 135). Even Lin seems a mixture, for "beyond his tallness" were "eyes that seemed the property of a not highly conscientious wild animal" (p. 143). Even though Wister sided with Westerners when comparing Lin with Easterners, he still wondered whether the Western experience was not a mixed blessing.

Now Wister had to make a decision. He had passed the bar examination, had become affiliated with a prestigious law firm, and had at least attempted to practice law. Yet during 1892 his first stories appeared in *Harper's Weekly* and *Harper's Monthly;* and his second book, *The Dragon of Wantley,* was published. Should he continue his law practice or should he turn to full-time writing? At first he could not make up his mind. His scrapbooks indicate that he was busy with the details of becoming a writer. He submitted his work to several magazines in order to broaden his markets. He wrote poems and essays on several subjects and turned out articles for newspapers. His actions indicate that probably some time during the year of 1892 he decided to become a Western writer. He reneged on a promise to write an article on the "Bar and Bench of Philadelphia," and he wrote and visited several editors in order to introduce them to his Western writings. Gradually, he turned to *Harper's.* Perhaps he settled there because he was rebuffed elsewhere; perhaps because *Harper's* was willing to pay handsomely for his work. It is evident that by early 1893 Wister was affiliated with *Harper's* and that they were giving his work special attention. So he had surmounted two difficult hurdles: his decision to become a writer, and his association with a well known and reliable publisher.

Wister moved quickly to solidify his position. He offered to write for *Harper's* a series of stories that would capitalize on the interest that readers had shown in his earlier Western fiction. At first the firm was reluctant, but by June of 1893 Alden wrote Wister: "Don't let any of your good things stray to our rivals— until you are dissatisfied with us" (Owen Wister Papers, June 15, 1893). Alden was aware that Wister was still flirting with other publishers, and the editor decided it was time to tie Wister to the *Harper's* publications. Within a month, he

18

and Wister had worked out a contract for a series of Western tales. There were to be eight stories, and they were to appear monthly from April to November 1894. Each story was to be about 7,500 words, and *Harper's* was willing to pay thirty-five dollars for a thousand words. The firm was attaching "more importance to it [the project] than to any of our undertakings of 1894" (Owen Wister Papers, July 14, 1893). As proof of *Harper's* willingness to hold to their bargain, Alden promised wide announcement of Wister's series, along with illustrations by Frederic Remington and publication of the stories in book form.

Wister was elated; he wrote his mother that the contract was "all that I could wish" (Owen Wister Papers, July 25, 1893). Now his work was laid out for him. He wrote several letters to his friends in the West and planned an itinerary that would carry him into new areas in order to gather materials for the projected series. If his first westward jaunts were for relaxation, those that occurred after the fall of 1893 were for the opposite purpose; now Wister went into the West as the gatherer of local color. His journals are full of notes about scenes he saw, about yarns he heard, and about stories he intended to produce from these raw materials.

The eight stories published as *Red Men and White* (November 1895) were written under the pressure of deadlines. Particularly was this so with the first five stories that Wister turned out between December 1893 and March 1894. If one expects Wister's best work in these short stories, he will be disappointed. They bear the brands of hurried composition.

Because *Harper's* was interested in fiction about Indians, Wister produced stories that centered on conflicts between the white and red races. "Little Big Horn Medicine," the first of the series, deals with Cheschapah, a young Crow who convinces himself and his followers of his invincibility and his power over nature. Though his elderly father, Pounded Meat, tries to talk sense to his son, the young brave is determined to defeat the soldiers stationed nearby and to chase them from the lands of the Crows. At first, nature seems to follow Cheschapah's will, and other young Indians champion his cause. But in battle his shield of invincibility disappears, and his reputation vanishes as quickly as a smoke signal.

Wister's story is not freighted with meaning. It is a tale of youthful arrogance that leads to destruction. More interesting is his view of the Indian as ignorant and superstitious—as a child easily led astray. Cheschapah fails because of his own ego and because he is too naive to understand the treacherous promises of a wily white trader. Wister implies that the fall of Cheschapah is not atypical; it is more likely to happen to the Indian. The young brave is a synecdochic figure; for Wister he symbolizes the weakness of his race. Wister speaks of the Indians as "crafty rabbits" and of the young brave as "the child whose primitive brain . . . . had been tampered with so easily" (pp. 11, 22).

Westerners like General Crook understand the nature of the Indians, but Easterners, "rancid with philanthropy and ignorance," comprehend little about the the red man. Too often, Wister says, "the superannuated cattle of the War Department sat sipping their drink at the club in Washington and explained to each other how they would have done it" (pp. 11, 113). In "The General's Bluff" Crook epitomizes the Western wisdom and bluff that are needed to survive in combat against the Indians—and against the stupidity of Eastern advisors.

Concurrent with his first attempts at picturing Indians is Wister's continued search for a Western hero. Here too Wister seems uncertain about what he wishes to say concerning the Western experience. Specimen Jones, a happy-go-lucky soldier, appears in three stories. In "Specimen Jones" he follows Jock Cumnor, a new recruit, through the desert and saves his life. Soon after they encounter the remains of an Apache ambush, they are confronted by the Indians. Specimen, realizing that their weapons are useless and drawing upon his understanding of red men's superstitions, begins to act as if he were crazy. He dances in drunken gyrations and pounds on an empty milk can. Specimen, who reminds one of some of the heroes of Eugene Manlove Rhodes, saves their lives because of his horse sense—a wisdom arising out of his Western experiences.

But Wister is not consistent in his portrayal of Specimen. In "The General's Bluff" he is the butt of several jokes and is more a good-natured and naive soldier than the wise, vernacular hero of "Specimen Jones." Then Wister changes again, and in "The Second Missouri Compromise" Specimen resumes his role as a Western wise man. He is portrayed as the shrewd but crude soldier who earns promotions because he knows what to do in times of crisis. Like Hemingway's heroes, he has a kind of "grace under pressure"; he knows *how* to act during crucial times. In this tale, Jones foreshadows the Virginian figure, for he has a folk wisdom that insures not only his own rise but also the safety of others. He drinks, carouses, and is a bit beyond polite society, but he has enough horse sense not to go to excess. He knows enough not to drink too much when he has responsibilities to carry out. As he says on one occasion, "If a man drinks much of that . . . he's liable to go home and steal his own pants" (p. 157). In the character of Specimen, Wister portrays a man who may become a man among men, but one who lacks the graces to be a satisfactory partner for the Eastern schoolmarm, and one who still falls short of encompassing much of what Wister thought the West did in shaping human character.

After Wister completed the first five stories, *Harper's* loosened its cinch and allowed him more time for the remaining three tales. "The Second Missouri Compromise," "La Tinaja Bonita," and "A Pilgrim on the Gila" were the most ambitious tales that Wister had produced thus far. Previously his stories were ones centering on an incident or two. His stress on character development was minimal, and he seemed little interested in using any social criticism. But in these three stories, Wister aims at a higher mark.

"A Pilgrim on the Gila" illustrates some of Wister's enlarged goals, and thus it contributes significantly to an understanding of his developing career. The plot is easily summarized. The narrator visits Washington, D.C., and hears arguments pro and con for the statehood of Arizona. Then he travels to Arizona and sees the Territory first hand. While in the area he meets several of the Territory's leading men, becomes involved (innocently) in a robbery, and plays a role in a subsequent trial. Based on the well-known Wham robbery and on Wister's personal observations, "A Pilgrim on the Gila" closely approximates the mood, form, and content of Wister's Western journals of 1894-95. The narrator, who poses as an onlooker and Eastern tenderfoot, resembles the spokesman in the opening pages of *The Virginian*. Like Wister in his journals, the narrator sees through the corrupt façade of Arizona's political, religious, and economic life. Third-rate politicians, religious bigots, and thieves run the Territory. Honest men are more scarce than untarnished women, and Tucson is a blight upon the land. The narrator is considered a naive tourist, but ironically it is he who comprehends the worthlessness of the Territorial society.

This story illustrates again Wister's divided response to the West. Though the region encouraged new opportunities, it also seemed to spawn, at times, mobocracy—democracy gone sour. Here mob rule disregards law and order and denies the rights of citizens. When the story appeared in *Harper's*, residents of the Territory criticized Wister for his distorted picture. Perhaps Arizona's being Democratic and Wister's being Republican made it easier for him to denigrate what he saw. His comments here are interesting prefigurements of the "Game and Nation" sections of *The Virginian*.

Concurrent with his work on the stories that were included

in *Red Men and White,* Wister was struggling with what is his most significant short piece of prose. Soon after his first Western trips, he began thinking of writing a history of the West which he titled tentatively "Course of Empire." In the early 1890's he broached the idea to Alden, but his editor encouraged him, instead, to undertake the stories included in *Red Men and White.* Then Wister was urged again to undertake his historical studies—this time by Frederic Remington, who told Wister he must chronicle the rise of the cowboy. This topic had intrigued Wister for some time, and in 1894 he began work on "The Evolution of the Cow-Puncher," which was published in September of 1895.

In the opening paragraph of the essay, Wister describes two Anglo Saxons—an English peer and an American—eyeing one another while they travel on an English train. Soon thereafter the Englishman, who dresses immaculately and displays the best drawing room manners, comes to Texas. The change is immediate.

> Directly the English nobleman smelt Texas, the slumbering untamed Saxon awoke in him, and mindful of the tournament, mindful of the hunting-field, galloped howling after wild cattle, a born horseman, a perfect athlete, and spite of the peerage and gules and argent, fundamentally kin with the drifting vagabonds who swore and galloped by his side. The man's outcome typifies the way of his race from the beginning. (p. 603)

As Ben Vorpahl has pointed out in *My Dear Wister,* the essay is not about the evolution of a type but about its continuation. The Westerner is little more than the medieval knight stripped of his older trappings.

> Destiny tried her latest experiment upon the Saxon, and plucking him from the library, the haystack, and the gutter, set him upon his horse; then it was that, face to face with the eternal simplicity of death, his modern guise fell away and showed once again the medieval man. It was no new type, no product of the frontier, but just the original kernel of the nut with the shell broken. (p. 610)

While the West did not produce the new type, it provided another testing ground for the Anglo Saxon—in this case the cattle country. Wister discusses briefly the clothing, the life-style, and the lingo of the cowpuncher, but he seems most interested in their racial qualities. In short, Wister admires the cowboy, and his admiration is heightened when he sees strong symbols of continuity between Anglo Saxon heroes of the past and those who now punch cows in the American West.

The story of the cowboy ends tragically. Though like other Anglo Saxons he "cuts the way for the common law and self government, and new creeds, politics, and nations arise in his wake," he also sows the seeds of his own destruction. He moves around too much, he never marries, and so he does not reproduce his own kind. "War they make in plenty, but not love; for the women they saw was not the woman a man can take into his heart" (p. 614). Progress—in the form of exhausted pastures, barbed-wire fences, and beef trusts—has pushed the cowboy aside. Wister laments his passing. Worst of all, as Wister notes, no poet has arisen yet to connect the man on horseback "with the eternal," and no skilled novelist has known the life of the cowboy sufficiently well "to lend him enchantment" (p. 605).

"The Evolution of the Cow-Puncher" summarizes Wister's ideas about race, reveals his view of the cowboy, and indicates his misgivings about the passing of the frontier and the coming of a new West. These three themes are central to an understanding of *The Virginian* and to an understanding of most of Wister's other Western fiction. And when he lamented that no writer had yet arisen to tell the story of the cowboy, he no doubt felt he was the man called out for that purpose. His friend Theodore Roosevelt thought so, and told Wister that the essay proved that he was now *the* writer of the cattle kingdom. Wister's most important Western fiction after the appearance of the essay in 1895 dealt with the themes mentioned above: the Anglo Saxon cowboy in a world that threatens to brush him aside unless he adapts to a rapidly-changing society.

As early as 1893, Wister outlined in his journals a series of stories that he wished to write about Lin McLean and the Virginian. At first, he thought of publishing separate stories about the two cowboys and then melting the episodes into a novel. Several occurrences kept him from carrying out his plans. The contract for the series that became *Red Men and White* put aside his plans for the Lin McLean-Virginian project for nearly two years. When he returned to the plan, there were other problems. By the end of 1895 he had written four stories in which Lin McLean appeared and several others in which the Virginian was either mentioned or played a major role. It was obvious, however, that not all the pieces would fit together. Wister realized he had two projects in the making, and he decided to add to the Lin McLean episodes in order to produce his first "novel." In 1897 the two remaining stories about Lin appeared, and the compilation of the six episodes was published as *Lin McLean* in late 1897.

Wister was disappointed—even disturbed—that reviewers of his novel stressed repeatedly its episodic nature. In an ill-humored "Preface" written for a 1907 edition of the book he argued that readers should have seen that the novel was "a chain of short stories, each not only a complete adventure in itself, but also a fragment of an underlying drama." Had the book been published in Europe—"where the writer is held as much accountable for his manner of saying a thing as for the thing he says"—critics would have noticed his "unusual device" for unifying the novel. Reluctantly admitting that his original form had not been entirely successful (in the eyes of reviewers), he allowed the new edition to be divided into chapters.

Wister hinted at the major flaw in *Lin McLean*. Attempting to publish sections of the book as separate stories and then trying to mold the stories into a well-knitted plot was a large order. The drawbacks of the plan are evident when parts of the book are examined. Soon after publishing "How Lin McLean Went East" in 1892, Wister formulated plans for the entire book. One year later the second section appeared as "The Winning of the Biscuit Shooter." This story details Lin's outsmarting of 'Rapaho Dick for the hand of Miss Katie Peck, former biscuit-shooter. In 1895, the third and fourth sections were published as "Lin McLean's Honeymoon" and "A Journey in Search of Christmas." The former tale is a humorous treatment of a rainmaker and of Lin's inability to keep his money and hence his wife, who gravitates to the cowpoke who wins Lin's stakes. Lin learns that Katie was previously married to the rainmaker's assistant (Lusk) and had married Lin without divorcing Lusk. The Christmas story tells of Lin's meeting Billy Lusk, son of Katie and her first husband, and of Lin's becoming the boy's sidekick during a Christmas shopping spree in Cheyenne.

The last two stories "Separ's Vigilante" and "Destiny at Drybone" were printed in 1897. "Separ's Vigilante" tells of the coming of Jessamine Buckner to the sagebrush hamlet of Separ. Billy Lusk and Lin, who has become the boy's protector, soon appear, and Lin is infatuated with Jessamine. He seems to be making headway until Billy tells her of Lin's unhappy union with Katie. The story ends abruptly with Jessamine's refusal of Lin's proposal; she will not accept a partner whose marital background contains other brands. "Destiny at Drybone" completes the tangled story of Lin's romances. Katie and Lusk reappear and Katie, depressed about her marital difficulties, takes an overdose of laudanum. Lin tries to save her, but she dies the next morning. When Lin returns to Jessamine and proposes again, she accepts. The tale ends with their returning to Lin's ranch.

Those who criticize the book's flimsy structure are correct. Several weaknesses are immediately perceptible. The first section was extensively revised before it appeared in the novel, and the revisions tightened an otherwise discursive narrative. But Wister failed to make other needed cuts. For example, "Destiny at Drybone" opens with a long conversation between Jessamine and Billy that brings readers up to date about happenings in the previous episodes. For the magazine appearance this introduction was necessary, but unfortunately Wister allowed these pages to remain in the book, where they are superfluous. Indeed, throughout the book there is evidence that Wister was either a careless or lazy editor. Had he taken the time and interest, he could have strengthened the structure of his book.

A second major problem is that of point of view. Some sections utilize a first person narrator; others employ an omniscient spokesman. Transitions between the two points of view are rough, and this unevenness frequently disrupts the tone of the novel. In the first parts the tone is flippant, and Lin is pictured as carefree and something of a picaro. But the last sections are increasingly contrived and sentimental. Wister seems uncertain about his hero. At first Lin seems free of responsibility, but gradually he becomes entangled in the demands of society. Yet Wister is reluctant to allow Lin to become civilized. Lin marries and seems to mature, but even in the last story he is pictured as both a responsible man and a "six-foot innocent." These problems of uneven form and muddled point of view are immediately noticeable in the book.

To stress only these problems, however, is to undervalue the novel. While few readers will agree with Jack Schaefer that it is Wister's best book, it is Wister's best accomplishment before the publication of *The Virginian*. *Lin McLean* is another dividing point in Wister's literary career. It illustrates the ideas and techniques that he has developed thus far, but it also demonstrates that he is still an uncertain artist when dealing with certain themes and character types.

In "The Evolution of the Cow-Puncher" Wister spoke about the passing of the cowboy. Now he had the opportunity to develop this theme. The opening sentence of *Lin McLean* pictures the West as a frontier that is vanishing. The story is set in "the old days, the happy days, when Wyoming was a Territory with a future instead of a State with a past, and the unfenced cattle grazed upon her ranges by prosperous thousands." Lin's maturation is portrayed against a West that is also growing up. As Lin falls in love and marries and then goes through the process once again, he moves from a young, irresponsible cowboy working for someone else to a man who owns a ranch. Meanwhile, the West is in transition from a frontier to a settled community. As Lin prospers, the West is dotted with towns, and the railroads appear. The movement, however, is not always straight forward. After his unsuccessful first marriage, Lin withdraws from society until another symbol of civilization—Jessamine Buckner—draws him out of hibernation. So it is with the civilizing of the West. Sometimes the frontier seems to live on, and society is brushed aside. The railroad attempts to keep a ticket agent and a much-needed watertank in Separ, but the cowboys enjoy "educating" the agent and perforating the tank with pistol shots. The narrator muses: "now what should authority do upon these free plains, this wilderness of do-as-you-please, where mere breathing the air was inebriation" (p. 158). Separ needed what Lin needed: a dose of civilizing. And, as is so often the case in Western American literature, the arrival of a woman—Jessamine—symbolizes the coming of settled so-

28

ciety. She calms the antics of the fun-loving cowpokes and domesticates the untamed heart of Lin McLean. She establishes a home in Lin's ranch house and takes command of Lin. His riding days are over.

In the final section of the novel, Wister describes at length what the passing of time does to Drybone. It has been an army post. But as the Indians are gradually killed off and "cattle by ten thousands came treading with the next step of civilization . . . the soldiers were taken away." A new society comes to replace that of the army post. The new residents include "every joy that made the cow-puncher's holiday, and every hunted person who was baffling the sheriff." A second childhood sets in, but in adolescence it already shows signs of old age. "Even in that day its hour could have been heard beginning to sound, but its inhabitants were rather deaf" (pp. 243, 245). Wister suits these descriptive passages to the action of his novel, for they prefigure the death of Katie. Like Drybone, she is unable to understand and cope with her destiny until it sweeps in upon her, and suicide seems the only way to avoid its inexorable pressures.

One final point about *Lin McLean,* a point that too few readers have noted. The novel is a finger exercise for *The Virginian.* In the story of Lin, Wister shoots for several goals that he aimed at again in his later novel. Lin's tale is one of his being domesticated and civilized by his love for a woman. Though Jessamine is a faint resemblance of Molly Wood, she serves a purpose similar to that of the New England schoolmarm. And *Lin McLean* is a novel about the West as it moves from frontier to region, a theme that is at the center of *The Virginian.* Finally, Wister experimented with the perspectives of two narrators, as he would in his most important novel. *Lin McLean* was Wister's first Western novel, and in the writing of it he learned several valuable lessons that he put to work in *The Virginian.*

Seen in this perspective, the earlier novel is an important step forward in Wister's apprenticeship as a Western writer.

In the two years following the appearance of *Lin McLean,* Wister did not publish a single Western story. He had other interests. In April of 1898 Wister married his distant cousin, Mary Channing Wister. Until her death in 1913, Mrs. Wister was a perfect partner. She shared her husband's interest in writing and in the other arts, and she handled well the affairs of a burgeoning household. In spite of these additional responsibilities, Mrs. Wister remained the soothing companion that her husband needed. Many years later Wister would say of his marriage: "There is but one piece of spiritual good fortune that surpasses having had the friendship of a great man, and that is to have had a perfect marriage" (*Roosevelt,* p. 58).

Following honeymoon trips to Charleston, South Carolina, and to the Methow Valley in the state of Washington, the Wisters settled into their home on Pine Street in Philadelphia, where they lived until 1908, when Wister's mother died and they moved to Butler Place. Though Wister published no Western stories during 1898 and 1899, he was working on several projects. Now that the tale of Lin McLean was completed, he turned again to the Virginian and worked sporadically on that story. In addition to this continuing project, Wister published four Western yarns in 1900, and these, joined with previously uncollected Western stories, were published as Wister's second collection of Western stories, *The Jimmyjohn Boss* (1900), which would be retitled *Hank's Woman* in the Collected Works Edition of 1928.

The collection is an uneven mix. The earlier stories are the weakest: "Hank's Woman" (1892), "The Promised Land" (1894), and "A Kinsman of Red Cloud" (1894). The latter two stories deal with Indians, but are too contrived and melodramatic to excite much interest. Wister claims to have based the yarns on actual occurrences—and his claims may be true—

but authenticity cannot atone for the unsatisfactory treatment of character and action these stories exhibit. Equally unconvincing is "Napoleon Shave-tail," which may have been so weak that Harper's would not publish it in one of its magazines.

Two other pieces in the collection—"Sharon's Choice" and "Twenty Minutes for Refreshments"—are meant to be humorous. The latter is the better of the two. Here the narrator is compelled to help judge a baby contest that includes entries from two towns, Sharon and Rincon. The contest is sponsored by a drummer who sells a baby food, Mrs. Eden's Manna. The drummer organizes the contest in such a way that in two categories all the mothers vote for their own babies for first prize, and hence no winner is chosen. But they unanimously support Manna-fed babies for second place, and these babies are awarded prizes. Competition for the third category nearly brings on a frontier civil war, and would have done so, except for the captivating speech of Shot-gun Smith, the father of twins, who persuades the judges that his offspring deserve first place. After arriving at the decision, the judges run for the waiting train and escape before they can be assaulted by the disappointed matrons. In "Twenty Minutes for Refreshments" Wister maintains a constant comic tone, develops the characters of several figures, and thus produces a successful humor sketch.

The final story, "Padre Ignazio," is the best story in this anthology. Here Wister abandons his usual setting of the cowboy West of the late Nineteenth Century and centers on California during the 1850's. The story of Padre Ignazio is one of reflection rather than action. The priest, who has served his California mission for twenty years, hungers and thirsts after good music and great books. When a young traveler, Gaston Villeré, visits the mission and tells of his recent journeys in Europe, the padre questions him long into the night about the latest European musical compositions and learns in amazement of Verdi's new opera, *Il Trovatore*. During the next few days, the priest confides in Gaston and tells him of his early years in Europe, of the loss of his wife and child, and of his decision to give his life in service as a missionary in the New World. Gaston does not realize how much his experiences tempt the priest to renounce his mission and to return to the Old World, where as a man of sixty he can live out his last years in the cultural atmosphere that he enjoys. After the young wanderer leaves for the gold fields, Padre Ignazio resolves to return to Europe when the next southward-sailing ship arrives. When the barkentine arrives and the priest begins to climb aboard, he is met by a stranger who delivers a letter and a bag of gold from Gaston. The letter relates that the young man struck it rich but sustained a mortal wound in an argument. On his deathbed he has written to the priest and tells him to use the gold to buy a new organ for the mission. Gaston's letter and request turn Padre Ignazio back to his mission. Thereafter he "remained cheerful master of the desires" to leave his duties.

By centering on the tensions within the priest, Wister develops one of his most persuasive characterizations. The padre struggles to avoid Temptation (the term he uses for the worldly appetites that Gaston whets), and yet he relishes his thoughts about Temptation. Padre Ignazio is caught between his earthly desires for a genteel European society and his heavenly mission of serving uncultural Western peasants. Wister used a similar conflict in "Hank's Woman" and would later utilize the clash between East (or Europe) and West in numerous other stories. In few of them does he develop the tensity as competently as he does in "Padre Ignazio." This brief piece is certainly one of Wister's best accomplishments, and it deserves more attention than it has received.

Reviewers paid little notice to *The Jimmyjohn Boss*—and rightly so. Most of the stories in the collection were second-rate performances, and only "Padre Ignazio" and perhaps "The Jimmyjohn Boss" and "Twenty Minutes for Refreshments" deserved praise. Wister may have been too busy to notice the reviewers' lack of interest. Early in 1900 he completed a brief biography of Ulysses S. Grant. It did not sell well in spite of Vice President Roosevelt's praise. Roosevelt wrote a note intended for use by Wister's publishers: "It seems to me that you have written the very best short biography which has ever been written of any prominent American. Indeed, I cannot now recall any volume of the same size as your's [sic] about any man of Grant's standing which comes as high" (Owen Wister Papers, March 11, 1901). Roosevelt was also supplying Wister with details for another tale about the Virginian, "The Game and Nation" (1900). The following year Wister turned out one Western story, "The Patronage of High Bear," for *Lippincott's,* and some articles about Roosevelt and wilderness hunting for *Outing.*

Meanwhile, he was working on his long-delayed novel of the Virginian. Early in 1902 the Wister family moved to Charleston where Wister worked diligently at completing his famous cowboy story. While Mrs. Wister served as an official representative from Pennsylvania to an exposition in Charleston, Wister labored at combining previously published stories about his hero with newly written sections that were needed to give his novel continuity. It was a difficult task and one that plagued Wister throughout the early months of 1902. But by April the project was finished, and the novel was published the next month.

The plot of *The Virginian* is so familiar that it needs but the briefest of summaries. Actually, the novel contains two overlapping story lines. First, it is a tale of the hero's rise from cowboy, to foreman, to ranch owner. His ascent is magnified via his conflicts with his major opponent, Trampas, as well as with rustlers, and with his own conscience. Alongside this story is another—that of romance. This narrative line is more complex because Molly Wood, the schoolmarm, is more than merely the heroine. She symbolizes the East and gentility as these forces move westward to civilize the frontier. By uniting these two plots, Wister synthesizes several elements of popular literature: the success of a good man, the defeat of a villain, the ennobling union of hero and heroine, and the unifying impact of a narrative that is fast-paced and easy to read. Equally important, Wister shared many Americans' yearning for a frontier that would not be lost; therefore his novel celebrates a Western life that appealed to many readers.

Wister's status as a writer of Western fiction rests primarily on his having written *The Virginian*. And so it should be, for the novel is his best Western work, illustrating several contributions that he made to the development of Western American literature.

In the first place, Wister was the first notable writer to utilize the cowboy as a literary hero. The cowboy had appeared in a few dime novels but nearly always as a minor figure and frequently in an ungallant role. In his earlier stories and in *Lin McLean* Wister had used cowboy heroes, but in *The Virginian* the cowboy becomes something new, a full-bodied romantic hero. He is not a working cowpoke; there are no scenes of roping, branding, and dehorning. The Virginian spends most of his time playing tricks, hunting thieves, and wooing Molly Wood. Indeed, Wister's protagonist is more than a cowboy. From the opening pages it is apparent that he is a breed apart:

> Lounging there at ease against the wall was a slim young giant, more beautiful than pictures. His broad, soft hat was pushed back; a loose-knotted, dull-scarlet handkerchief sagged from his throat; and one casual thumb was hooked in the cartridge-belt that slanted across his hips. . . . The weather-beaten bloom of his face shone through it duskily, as the ripe peaches look upon their trees in a dry season. But no dinginess of travel or shabbiness of attire could tarnish the splendor that radiated from his youth and strength.

The Virginian is a bit uncouth, but the Eastern heroine gentles him. She rounds off his rough corners by reading Browning and Shakespeare to him. As the heroine she is attractive and pristine and succumbs to his gentle ways only after she has endured a good deal of indecision. In joining the Virginian (West) and Molly (East), Wister employs a popular technique used in many dime novels about the West. In fact, as Wallace Stegner has pointed out, a major theme in literature of the West is the conflict between the Virginian figure, who represents rawness, individualism, and democracy, and the Eastern symbol, which is usually feminine, educated, and genteel. Not all Western writers go as far as Wister and unite the two symbols, but this union particularly suited the sentiments of Wister.

The figure of the Virginian has meaning beyond the West. Wister was convinced that the West offered America its best opportunity—and perhaps its last—to hold on to the traditional virtues of democracy, individualism, and Anglo-Saxonism. So Wister's Virginian is a Westerner but also an American. He is the ideal fulfillment of the nostalgic mood that Wister and his friends shared about the past. Wister's cowboy is the strong individual, the frontiersman, the bringer of law and order. He symbolizes two things: an attachment to an older America, and a bulwark against a rising tide of southern European immigrants, whom many men of Wister's time welcomed like a sheepman moving into cattle country.

The Virginian helped to establish the conventions of what has become known as the "formula Western." Wister's skillful blending of an idealized hero, the conflict between the hero and a villain, and the romance between the hero and heroine—all set against the romantic background of the frontier West—are important ingredients of the Western. Because the novel was immensely popular and because it capitalized on the era's interest in the West, several other authors—mostly of lesser talent than Wister—imitated the formula of *The Virgin-*

ian. Zane Grey, Max Brand, and B. M. Bower began to turn out dozens of Western stories that followed closely the mixture of action, love, and good vs. evil that Wister utilized. Most of their efforts were inferior to *The Virginian,* but because Wister's novel seemed to start the avalanche of formula Westerns, this author has received more than his share of undeserved condemnation. He has been, to coin a term, a victim of hindsight criticism. Too often dude critics, looking back with the 20-20 vision of more than half a century and seeing all the literary fantasy written about the West, have pointed the finger of guilt at Wister for starting it all. Doing so is like blaming James Fenimore Cooper for the worthless dime novels written about pioneers and Indians, or like castigating Edgar Allan Poe for all that has claimed to be detective fiction. Wister could have written sequels to *The Virginian* and thereby could have capitalized on his name, his cowboy hero, and the West; but he chose not to do so. In one sense, then, Wister was an introducer—the writer who presented the cowboy to popular fiction and the man who brought together in one novel the necessary ingredients for the formula of the Western. He helped create a fictional hero and a popular literary genre whose places in the American pantheon are as secure as mother and apple pie.

But to see *The Virginian* only as the first Western is to miss other major contributions of the work. The novel also illustrates Wister's continued ambiguous response to the West. Though his journals and his earlier stories and essays give one scattered glimpses of Wister's ambivalence about the West, it is in *The Virginian* that one sees the fullest perspective of the dilemma—and perhaps Wister's resolution of his conflicting attitudes.

As we have seen, Wister was convinced that the West produced such manly specimens as the Virginian. At the same time, other happenings in the novel indicate that Wister is still doubtful about the frontier's being entirely beneficial to men. For example, Balaam, the rancher who mistreats horses, is an Easterner who comes West, and Wister implies that the frontier encourages his brutality and inhumanity. Even the Virginian falls victim to pressures toward violence. He hurls Balaam to the ground and beats him severely about the face after Balaam has mistreated a horse. The Virginian is the law-bringer, but he is also a man of violence. Though he is nature's nobleman, he also participates in lynching, gun-fighting, and perhaps wenching. So the image of the hero is blurred—a strong individual and yet a violent one. He is Wister's untamed gentleman.

In addition, *The Virginian* also demonstrates some of the cultural tensions of the era. The novel is a reflection of its times. It epitomizes the duality of the progressive mind. The temper of the times was both forward-looking and backward-looking. At first, the most apparent pull in Wister's novel is his attachment to the West as the old frontier. His hero seems to come straight out of pre-Carnegie and pre-Rockefeller days. Self-reliant, individualistic, and freedom-loving, he is Frederick Jackson Turner's frontiersman in his leather-fringed jacket of democracy. At the same time, though most of the novel pictures the hero as the epitome of individualism and freedom, he gradually moves in another direction—toward marriage, toward a part in society, and eventually toward another alliance—with the machine. So the novel ends with the Virginian accepting the railroads, accepting his new responsibilities in a post-frontier society. Though his son will continue to ride his father's horse, the hero takes up with the machine which steams into his territory. The ending of *The Virginian* is Owen Wister's testament of acceptance. Like many other men of the progressive era, Wister came to terms with industrialism and accepted the likelihood of its dominance. Though he would continue to long for wide-open spaces and for the symbolic old West, he turned to the machine as a key to the future of America.

With the publication of *The Virginian*, Wister's career as a Western writer reached its apex. The novel was his best work about the West and was certainly his most popular. Never again was he able to excite his readers as he had done in *The Virginian*.

Members of the Family (1911) collected nearly all the Western stories which Wister had written between 1901 and 1911. Most of the stories appeared first in *Cosmopolitan* and *Saturday Evening Post* and strongly reflect Wister's changing feelings about the West. The introduction to the volume indicates Wister's awareness that the region had changed. He says: "The nomadic, bachelor West is over, the housed, married West is established." And then he adds: "I own to an attachment for the members of this family; I would fain follow their lives a little more, into twentieth century Wyoming, which knows not the cow-boy, and where the cow-boy feels at times more lost than ever he was on the range" (pp. 10, 21). Our old friends are reintroduced: the Virginian, Lin McLean, Scipio Le Moyne, Uncle Pasco, and the tenderfoot narrator; but their world has changed—both in time and mood.

Wister's ambivalence about the West—so unmistakable in his stories of the 1890's and in *The Virginian*—is not evident in these later pieces. Perhaps this is because a happy marriage, a satisfactory occupation, and a mounting income assuaged his earlier personal tensions. Perhaps too the ambiguity lessened because he no longer saw the region as caught between the old and the new; the frontier had closed. Wister still writes about the frontier period, but now the mood is primarily one of nostalgia. In the final story of the collection, the omniscient narrator intrudes to say that times have changed, that too many people have moved in. "When Wyoming was young and its ranches lay wide, desert miles apart, such hospitality was the natural, unwritten law; but now, in this day of increasing settlements and of rainbowed folders of railroads painting a promised land for all comers, a young ranchman could easily be kept poor by the perpetual drain on his groceries and oats" (p. 286).

Wister's changed feelings about the West are obvious in both the form and mood of his tales. For example, he makes less use of the first person narrator, who had served as a chorus in his previous stories. The "I" figure does not play a prominent role in *Members of the Family*; he rarely comments at length on the action or on other characters; and thus Wister misses the opportunity to make use of the rites-of-passage theme utilized in *The Virginian*. An exception is "The Gift Horse" in which the initiation of the narrator is superbly portrayed.

Closely related to the diminished importance of the "I" figure is Wister's inability (or unwillingness) to stress conflicts between East and West. In the opening tale Horace (Horacles) Pericles Bynam, an Easterner, fails in his goal to undermine the Agent's monopoly on sales to the Indians. Scipio, who works for the Agent, outsmarts Horacles because the latter does not understand the child-like, innocent Indians—though Scipio (the Westerner) does. But Wister is unable to portray Horacles as a believable representative of an alien Eastern culture; and so his battles with Scipio are not persuasive East-West conflicts. Throughout these stories Scipio comes closest to being a symbol of the West, and at times he seems to represent Western vernacular values, but his viewpoint is not sufficiently sustained to make him as convincing a character as Lin McLean or the Virginian.

Because for Wister the West had changed—physically and psychologically—one notes a different mood in his stories. He no longer hints at the West's being the region of promise; in fact, the idea is not even introduced. And on the other hand, Wister does not emphasize the vulgar and brutalizing aspects of Western experience that he mentioned earlier. The West, as frontier or region, seems to have lost much of its meaning for Wister, and hence his writings contain less social commentary about the West.

Most of the stories of *Members of the Family* are short sketches or tales consisting of a single episode. "Spit-Cat Creek" tells of Scipio's ability to outsmart Uncle Pasco, who tries to rob him of a large sum of money. "Timberline" is a yarn about a hunting trip Scipio and the narrator take into the mountains. They take along as a cook a ne'er-do-well named Timberline. When they are caught in an electric storm high up in the Washakie Needles, Timberline admits his part in two previous murders and (befuddled by the lightning-charged air) jumps over a cliff. While based partially on an experience Wister had in 1888, the story has little literary significance. "Extra Dry" is the story of Bellyful, a young man without a job and nearly destitute. While in town one day, he watches a shell game shyster and his cohorts separate a man from his money. Bellyful leaves town, and then on the spur of the moment he decides to rob the shell game man. He takes the money and goes on his way. Scipio tells the story, and when the "I" narrator ventures to criticize Bellyful, Scipio reveals that he was Bellyful and argues that since his actions were not wrong he is not sorry for them. He will not let the narrator change any of the story's details if he wishes to write about the incident. These three stories are sketches; they contain little plot or attempt at characterization. While Wister includes some lively dialogue and a few paragraphs of apt description, the tales do not rank with his best work.

Two other yarns are much better. As mentioned above, "The Gift Horse" is a sensitive treatment of the first person narrator's initiation into maturity. He learns some differences between appearances and realities. Late in the story he becomes aware that he has befriended a rustler whose activities lead the narrator straight into a vigilante trap. Only the coincidental return of Scipio at just the right moment to save the narrator mars an otherwise convincing portrayal of a *bildungsroman* story. "The Drake Who Had Means of His Own" is a delightful yarn in which conflicts between a drake and two of his hens are paralleled with a battle for dominance in a new marriage. The narrator wonders how the drake keeps the hens under such tight control; so too is he mystified about the struggles between the newlyweds, May and Jimsey. He tells Jimsey about the drake, and the young bridegroom immediately perceives the "means" of the drake. Jimsey tells the narrator the drake's secret: "Has 'em competin' for him. Keeps 'em a guessing. That's his game." And it is obvious that Jimsey now knows how to handle his bride. Although containing little significance, the story is an entertaining and humorous yarn. In fact, the story illustrates Wister's approach in this collection: sketches or tales that utilize humor or melodrama to emphasize incident more than character or theme.

After the publication of *Members of the Family* in 1911, Wister did not write another Western story until 1924. For nearly thirteen years Wister was tied to other interests. Though he purchased a ranch in the vicinity of Jackson Hole, Wyoming, and made several trips to that area, he became more involved in events that led to the First World War. Gradually, he turned again to Europe, and his daughter tells us that after his wife's death in 1913 and whenever the absence of hostilities allowed him to do so, he loved to wander through the European countryside studying the cathedrals and testing the latest wines. In short, Wister became less and less attached to the West and more and more attracted to the East and to Europe. It is within this perspective that one must view his last Western stories. Written between 1924 and 1928, these nine tales (all but one of which was first published in *Cosmopolitan*) were collected in 1928 as *When West Was West*.

Several of the problems typical of *Members of the Family* plague Wister in his later stories. "Bad Medicine," the first piece in *When West Was West*, is an unconvincing portrayal of Sun Road, a Shoshone chief, who undergoes a dramatic change of character. At first he will not allow tourists to photograph him, but by the end of the story he actually enjoys posing. Wister's treatment of the chief's rapid change of feeling is not persuasive. The portrait of Sun Road is, at best, muddled. The next story, "Captain Quid," aims at satirizing gossipy officers' wives, but it is too rambling and wordy to accomplish its goal.

Wister's satire is sharper in other pieces that deal with the Southwest. In "Once Around the Clock" Doc Leonard, a young physician recently graduated from Harvard, tries to set up practice in Texas, but he finds that the people of the area flock to Professor Salamanca, a middle-aged quack woman doctor who spends much of her time with young male "associates." As the plot zips along, several of the Professor's sidekicks are killed off because they seem treasonous to her evil designs. Leonard's only ally, Colonel Steptoe McDee, keeps the young doctor out of trouble, warns him of the Professor's wilyness, and tells him to leave after his life is threatened. There the story ends—abruptly and without purpose. "Skip to My Loo," the only piece in the collection not to appear first in a magazine, is Wister's harshest denunciation of Texans and of what he considers their basic hypocrisy. The story tells of a Negro pimp who arranges for a returning rancher's night of entertainment at a local brothel. Meanwhile, the rancher's wife, thinking her husband will not return for a day or two, takes her regular turn at the sporting house. As one might suspect, the panderer brings together man and wife in these strange circumstances. Doc Leonard, who narrates the story, tells of hearing a shot and of rushing to the scene to find the Negro dead from a gunshot. Later, after the narrator puts the pieces of the ironic puzzle together, he returns to the rancher's house and finds the couple together. They act as if nothing unusual has happened.

These tales and "Little Old Scaffold" were based on stories that Wister heard in Texas and recorded in his journals. But when he came to transposing the stories into fiction he had difficulty. None of his characters is well drawn, and his purposes are too explicit. As Wister pointed out earlier in his introduction to *Red Men and White,* he was disgusted with the hypocrisy of Texans. Their towns were free from trash and disorder, and they denounced dancing as a terrible evil. And they even criticized men for speaking of *stallions* and *boars* in the presence of women. Yet behind these false fronts, they were the worst kind of racists, adulterers, and even murderers. Wister's point of view is clear and explicit, but he is unable to translate his ideas into well-conceived characters and smooth narratives.

Fortunately, two of the remaining stories are among the best Wister produced. Both stories are first rate. The stronger of the two is "The Right Honorable the Strawberries," a tale based on material that Wister had obtained in Wyoming in the 1890's. An Englishman appears unannounced in Drybone, Wyoming, and his friendly, winsome ways garner him many friends. He is soon nicknamed Strawberries, and one cowboy, Chalkeye, becomes so attached to the newcomer that he serves as his mentor and protector. Strawberries learns the ways of the cattle country and seems to become a real cowpoke. Later on, another titled Englishman and an old acquaintance of Strawberries—Lord Deepmere—arrives and immediately snubs Strawberries, who soon thereafter begins a moral decline. He takes up cards, drinks heavily, and lives unmarried with a woman. His downward slide leads him to cheating at cards. Then Chalkeye learns of a plot to kill Strawberries. Chalkeye works a plan to save Strawberries and to send him away from Drybone, but in protecting his friend he loses his own life. The closing scene brings together the "I" narrator and Strawberries after many years. They talk of old times and agree that Chalkeye was a man among men.

One interpreter—Neal Lambert—points to this story as Wister's "final assessment" of the "values of the frontier." He contends that Wister realized that the East (symbolized by the

Englishman) and the frontier were incompatible. Though Strawberries appears to become a Westerner, he never really makes the transition, and a major reason for his failure and his final downfall is that his set of values is not compatible with those of Chalkeye and the other cowboys. Lambert's point is well taken; the story is indeed centered on the conflict between two incongruous sets of values. Wister makes the conflict believable because he creates three superb characters—the narrator, Strawberries, and Chalkeye. The actions of these men are well motivated—hence the plot is believable. There are no unnecessary scenes or excessive dialogue—two weaknesses of the other later stories. Finally there is a strong sense of a West that is gone—a Past that the narrator and Strawberries remember in the figure of Chalkeye.

"At the Sign of the Last Chance," the final story in *When West Was West,* is Owen Wister's requiem for the frontier. The narrator returns to an old haunt that is little more than a ghost town. He finds several men who are relics from the past and who are living out the remainder of their lives in this isolated spot. He joins them in an old saloon for a night of cards, and they talk of old times—times that were obviously lively and free compared to their present dull and depressing existence. They are reminded of an old custom of burying the sign of a saloon that has given up the ghost. They carry out the symbolic act in the last scene of the story.

Unlike the story of Strawberries, this yarn centers on feeling and mood rather than on character and conflict of values. There is no plot, and none of the characters is finely etched. But Wister persuasively describes what the passing of time has done to the frontier. Here is a picture of a frontier that is nearly deceased—that can be revived only in memories of men who have outlived their era. The New West has passed them by. Although this is not Wister's best story, its theme and mood are a fitting conclusion to his career as a Western writer. The story rivals Walter Van Tilburg Clark's "The Wind and Snow of Winter" as a first-rate portrait of an Old West that has disappeared. As such, the story deserves a place among the best half dozen shorter pieces that Wister wrote.

So ended the career of Owen Wister as a Western writer. His output of Western materials was not large: the journals, four collections of short stories, two medium-length novels, and a few uncollected short pieces. Most of his Western writing was produced in one decade. From 1892 to 1902 he showed consistent growth, and it was during this era that his best work appeared. After that time, he turned out only four or five stories worthy of notice.

Wister was not a first-rate writer; his writings do not belong on a list of America's best fiction. At times he showed signs of becoming an important fictionist, but he was unwilling to break the strands that tied him to the demands of popular magazine fiction. Had he been more willing—as Stephen Crane, Theodore Dreiser, and Frank Norris were—to forgo the financial rewards of magazine appearance, he would have been allowed more freedom of subject matter and treatment. In addition, Wister gives too few signs of being a serious student of his craft; too often his longer pieces show careless revision and unnecessary padding. And he too easily followed the advice of men like William Dean Howells and Theodore Roosevelt even when he disagreed with their judgments. In short, Wister was boxed in by his backgrounds and his prejudices; these albatrosses were major reasons why he did not achieve more as a writer.

In the development of Western American fiction Wister occupies a middle position. Though he wrote more realistically about the West than previous dime novelists and was a better craftsman than some of his contemporaries—Alfred Henry Lewis and Andy Adams, for example—he does not merit a place alongside superior Western novelists like Willa Cather, John Steinbeck, H. L. Davis, Walter Van Tilburg Clark, and Wallace

Stegner. His understanding of Western experiences and of their shaping influences upon character is not nearly as profound as that illustrated in the regional writing of Cather, Clark, or Wright Morris. Wister was a better yarn-spinner, a sketcher of episodes, than a superb creator of character or a student of form. He did not come to grips sufficiently with how a region could brand its unique ways into the hides of its natives.

In several respects, then, Wister is a more important figure for the literary and cultural historian than he is for the student of American belles lettres. He reflects a great deal of his era and its attitudes toward the West. Like Mary Hallock Foote, Helen Hunt Jackson, and Frederic Remington, he was a genteel Easterner who came into the West in the last years of the Nineteenth Century and who wrote about the ending of the frontier. Had he worked harder at his craft, he might have given us a first-rate novel centering on the pivotal period between the ending of the frontier and the beginning of the modern West. Wister did not give us this much-needed portrait, but he and his writings do give us extraordinary insight into the feelings and moods of the progressive Era and its attitudes about the West. For this reason alone, the Western work of Owen Wister is worthy of continued study.

Selected Bibliography

For complete lists of works by Wister see the bibliographies by Sherman and Weber listed below. Professor Sanford Marovitz is preparing an exhaustive bibliography of commentary on Wister's writings that will appear soon in *American Literary Realism.* The Owen Wister Papers are in The Library of Congress.

Western Works by Owen Wister

BOOKS

Red Men and White. New York: Harper & Brothers, 1896.

Lin McLean. New York: Harper & Brothers, 1897.

The Jimmyjohn Boss and Other Stories. New York: Harper & Brothers, 1900.

The Virginian: A Horseman of the Plains. New York: The Macmillan Company, 1902.

Members of the Family. New York: The Macmillan Company, 1911.

When West Was West. New York: The Macmillan Company, 1928.

The Writings of Owen Wister. 11 vols. New York: The Macmillan Company, 1928.

Roosevelt: The Story of a Friendship, 1880-1919. New York: The Macmillan Company, 1930.

Owen Wister Out West: His Journals and Letters. Ed. Frances Kemble Wister. Chicago: University of Chicago Press, 1958.

ESSAYS AND POEMS

"Autumn on Wind River." *Harper's New Monthly Magazine,* 94 (April 1897), 774 (poem).

"Concerning Bad Men: The True 'Bad Man' of the Frontier, and the Reasons for His Existence." *Everybody's Magazine,* 4 (April 1901), 320-28 (essay).

"Educating the Polo Pony." *Outing,* 36 (June 1900), 296-99 (essay).

"An Electric Storm on the Washakie Needles." *Science,* 28 (December 11, 1908), 837-39 (essay).

"The Evolution of the Cow-Puncher." *Harper's New Monthly Magazine,* 91 (September 1895), 602-17 (essay).

"The Mountain Sheep: His Ways" and "The White Goat and His Ways." *Musk Ox, Bison, Sheep and Goat.* Ed. George Bird Grinnell and Caspar Whitney. New York: Macmillan Company, 1904. Pp. 167-273 (essays).

"Old Yellowstone Days." *Harper's Magazine,* 172 (March 1936), 471-80 (essay).

"The White Goat and His Country." *American Big Game Hunting.* New York: Forest and Stream Publishing Company, 1893. Pp. 26-60 (essay).

"Wilderness Hunter." *Outing,* 39 (December 1901), 250-55 (essay).

Manuscripts and Forthcoming Publications

Important collections of manuscript materials concerning Wister are deposited in the Library of Congress, New York Public Library, University of Wyoming Library, and the Harvard University Library. Professors George Watkins, Neal Lambert, and Ben Vorpahl are preparing full-length studies of Wister.

Bibliographies

Etulain, Richard W. *Western American Literature: A Bibliography of Interpretive Books and Articles.* Vermillion: Dakota Press, 1972. Pp. 134-36. (Lists unpublished dissertations and theses dealing with Wister.)

Sherman, Dean. "Owen Wister: An Annotated Bibliography." *Bulletin of Bibliography,* 28 (January-March 1971), 7-16.

Weber, Richard Charles. "Owen Wister: An Annotated Bibliography." Unpublished master's thesis, University of Northern Iowa, 1971.

Works About Wister

Barsness, John A. "Theodore Roosevelt as Cowboy: The Virginian as Jacksonian Man." *American Quarterly,* 21 (Fall 1969), 609-19.

Boatright, Mody C. "The American Myth Rides the Range: Owen Wister's Man on Horseback." *Southwest Review,* 36 (Summer 1951), 157-63.

Bode, Carl. "Henry James and Owen Wister." *American Literature,* 26 (May 1954), 250-52.

Durham, Philip. "Introduction" and "Textual Note." *The Virginian.* Riverside Edition. Boston: Houghton Mifflin Company, 1968.

Etulain, Richard. "Origins of the Western." *Journal of Popular Culture,* 4 (Fall 1970), 518-26.

Frantz, Joe B. and Julian Ernest Choate, Jr. *The American Cowboy: The Myth and the Reality.* Norman: University of Oklahoma Press, 1955.

Houghton, Donald E. "Two Heroes in One: Reflections Upon the Popularity of *The Virginian.*" *Journal of Popular Culture,* 4 (Fall 1970), 497-506.

Hubbell, Jay B. "Owen Wister's Work." *South Atlantic Quarterly,* 29 (1930), 440-43.

Lambert, Neal. "Owen Wister's 'Hank's Woman': The Writer and His Comment." *Western American Literature,* 4 (Spring 1969), 39-50.

———. "Owen Wister's Lin McLean: The Failure of the Vernacular Hero." *Western American Literature,* 5 (Fall 1970), 219-32.

———. "Owen Wister's Virginian: The Genesis of a Cultural Hero." *Western American Literature,* 6 (Summer 1971), 99-107.

———. "The Values of the Frontier: Owen Wister's Final Assessment." *South Dakota Review,* 9 (Spring 1971), 76-87.

Lewis, Marvin. "Owen Wister: Cast Imprints in Western Letters." *Arizona Quarterly,* 10 (Summer 1954), 147-56.

Rush, N. Orwin. "Frederic Remington and Owen Wister: The Story of Friendship." *Probing the American West.* Ed. K. Ross Toole, *et al.* Santa Fe: Museum of New Mexico Press, 1962.

Stokes, Frances Kemble Wister. *My Father, Owen Wister, and Ten Letters Written by Owen Wister to his Mother during his First Trip to Wyoming in 1885.* Laramie: University of Wyoming Library Associates, 1952.

Vorpahl, Ben M. "Henry James and Owen Wister." *The Pennsylvania Magazine of History and Biography,* 95 (July 1971), 291-338.

———. "Ernest Hemingway and Owen Wister." *Library Chronicle,* 36 (Spring 1970), 126-37.

———. *My Dear Wister: The Frederic Remington-Owen Wister Letters.* Palo Alto: American West Publishing Company, 1972.

Walker, Don D. "Essays in the Criticism of Western Literary Criticism: II.

The Dogmas of DeVoto." *The Possible Sack* [University of Utah], 3 (November 1971) , 1-7.

———. "Wister, Roosevelt and James: A Note on the Western." *American Quarterly,* 12 (Fall 1960) , 358-66.

White, G. Edward. *The Eastern Establishment and the Western Experience: The West of Frederic Remington, Theodore Roosevelt, and Owen Wister.* New Haven: Yale University Press, 1968.

White, John I. "The Virginian." *Montana Magazine of Western History,* 16 (October 1966) , 2-11.

Wister, Fanny K. "Letters of Owen Wister, Author of *The Virginian.*" *The Pennsylvania Magazine of History and Biography,* 83 (January 1959) , 3-28.

———. "Owen Wister's West." *Atlantic Monthly,* 195 (May 1955) , 29-35; (June 1955) , 52-57.

Wister, Owen. "Strictly Hereditary." *Musical Quarterly,* 22 (January, 1936) , 1-7.